TELL ME A MITZVAH

Little and Big Ways to Repair the World

DANNY SIEGEL

Pictures by Judith Friedman

KAR-BEN COPIES, INC.   ROCKVILLE, MD

To my courageous, strong,
and generous sister
Leslye

חיה אסתר

My Teacher

And to some of my chevra
from the good old days in USY
Mark Stadler, Marci Brumberg,
Steve Kahan, and David Kaplan
Good Friends, Sweet Rebbis
All of Them

Library of Congress Cataloging-in-Publication Data

Siegel, Danny
    Tell me a mitzvah/Danny Siegel: illustrated by Judith Friedman.
      p.   cm.
    Summary: Recounts the mitzvahs, or good deeds, of a dozen men and women and
suggests ways young people can help others.
    ISBN 0-929371-78-X (pbk.):
    1. Commandments (Judaism)—Juvenile literature. 2. Jewish children—Conduct of
life—Juvenile literature. 3. Ethics, Jewish—Juvenile literature. 4. Jewish way of life—
Juvenile literature. [1. Commandments (Judaism) 2. Ethics, Jewish. 3. Charity.
4. Conduct of life.] I. Friedman, Judith, ill. II. Title.
BM520.7.S53 1993
296.3'85—dc20   93-7552
                                                      CIP
                                                      AC

J256
SieT

CONTENTS

INTRODUCTION

This book is about mitzvahs, the simple yet sublime kind deeds that people do for others. And it is about mitzvah heroes, the men, women, and children who personify the intensity and extent of mitzvahs in our world today. The word *mitzvah* (plural, *mitzvot*) technically means commandment, and refers to the entire range of God's commandments that are written in the Torah, the first five books of the Bible. These include observing the Sabbath and holidays, keeping the dietary laws (*kashrut*), and providing for the sick, the aged, and the orphan. I use the word *mitzvah* in this book, however, as a synonym for personal acts of goodness, and I have chosen the Yiddish plural, *mitzvahs*, because it traditionally connotes these wonderful deeds.

A Note of Gratitude

I am grateful to my friends who tested some of these stories with their children and students. I particularly thank the 1992 fifth and sixth grade classes of the Donna Klein Jewish Academy, Boca Raton, FL, whose personal critiques gave me the greatest encouragement.

Also — as always — my thanks to my mother, Edythe Siegel, for her proofreading and suggestions as *Tell Me a Mitzvah* took shape.

THE WOMAN WITH A
VERY SMALL KITCHEN

It would take me a long time to count how many synagogues I've visited. I think it's about 300. Some were big with very high ceilings. Some had beautiful windows with all kinds of colored glass that told stories about Abraham and Sarah, and Moses on Mt. Sinai.

One had huge windows that looked out on a big lake, and at another — up in Alaska — sometimes you could see a moose running across the lawn. But this story is about a very small synagogue in Jerusalem, on a not-so-big street called Joseph Caro Street, with a very small kitchen next door.

The synagogue has space for 25 or 30 people to sit, but in the kitchen, four people is a crowd, and you have to say, "Excuse me," if you want to go over to the sink or refrigerator or stove. Even the doorway is small, and I have to bend down a little before going in.

Now inside this kitchen is a cook whose name is Tova. She isn't even five feet tall. But this very small woman in this very small kitchen manages to cook great quantities of food for the people next door at the synagogue.

Every Wednesday morning, for years and years, Tova has gotten up really early in the morning — sometimes as early as 4 a.m. — to cook for the old peo-

ple who come to study Torah, and for others who come just to visit and chat and sit on the little porch outside. Some are in their 80's or 90's; some are maybe 100-years old.

Even when I am a block away from Tova's kitchen, I can smell the wonderful food she cooks — soup and chicken and vegetables, all with lots of spices, because Tova and the old people are from places like Iran and Yemen, where they like spicy food.

Whenever I see Tova, she is always smiling, even if it's hot outside, and hotter inside the kitchen. I don't think she even notices the heat, because she is so happy to be doing a mitzvah.

Some of the people who come are poor, and some might be a lot hungrier if it weren't for Tova's wonderful Wednesday meal. Others have enough to eat at home, but are hungry for friendship. You can't tell which ones are which, and that's the way Tova likes it. Whoever wants may come and eat.

When the old people thank her, Tova looks away embarrassed because she thinks you don't need to be thanked for doing a mitzvah. It is enough that people are enjoying a good meal, and if it gives some of them more strength to study Torah, that makes her even happier.

Sometimes when I go to one of those lox and bagel brunches in a synagogue in Chicago or New York or Boston, I close my eyes and think of the little synagogue in Jerusalem with the tiny kitchen next door. I can smell the soup and the chicken and rice and the nice desserts Tova is making for the old people and it reminds me that there are mitzvahs to be done everywhere and all the time.

What Can I Do?

THE TUNA FISH MITZVAH

If someone asked you to bake 427 brownies or 67 devil's food cakes for a bake sale to raise money for tzedakah, you might say, "Well that's too difficult a mitzvah."

But other mitzvahs don't take any time at all and after awhile they can make a big difference.

Every time you are at the supermarket, remember to pick out one extra thing to give away. It can be a box of cereal, a jar of peanut butter or a can of tuna. It can even be a bottle of shampoo or a tube of toothpaste.

Some people think this kind of mitzvah is for grown-ups, but it isn't. Children should do it, too, and if they do it every time they are in a store, they'll keep doing it when they're grown-ups.

And it isn't the kind of mitzvah that only grown-ups should pay for. Remember to take a nickel or a dime or a quarter with you when you go shopping, so that when you get to the check-out counter, you can pay for at least part of what you bought.

It's easy to get into the mitzvah habit, especially if you think about the hungry people who won't be quite so hungry, because you took a minute to remember them and to do something about it.

THE WOMAN WHO HAD
70,000 PAIRS OF SHOES

Once upon a time, Ranya Kelly of Denver had 70,000 pairs of shoes.

She doesn't own a shoe store or department store, and she doesn't keep them for herself. She gives them away.

Some years ago, Ranya wanted to send a present to someone, but she didn't have a box big enough. So she went to a shopping center and looked in the big dumpsters behind the stores. She knew that grocery stores and department stores throw away lots of boxes and cartons.

When she looked through the side door of one of the really big dumpsters she was surprised to see shoes. Many, many shoes. By the end of the day, she counted about 500 pairs.

Ranya couldn't tell why these shoes were being thrown away. They looked all right to her. So she called her husband and told him to drive over, and she climbed inside the dumpster and started handing him the shoes. There were so many shoes, they had to take a vanful home, unload, and come back for a second batch.

What could she do with so many shoes? She took some for her family, gave some away to relatives and friends, and still there were hundreds of pairs left.

Then, Ranya went to a local shelter for homeless people in town and started to give away more shoes. She had never been to a shelter, and she was very sad to see so many people who didn't have decent shoes to wear. That's when she decided to keep looking in the dumpsters.

As she kept finding more and more perfectly good shoes, she tried to convince the stores to give her the shoes instead of throwing them away. At first they wouldn't listen, but finally they agreed.

Now she and her friends go to the shoe stores and pick up shoes and boots and slippers and sandals and sneakers and baby shoes — all kinds of shoes — and give them away.

As people began to hear about Ranya and her shoes, stores began to call her when they were about to throw things in dumpsters — blankets with a little dirt stain, a doll whose voice didn't work, dresses or shirts with buttons missing, or perfectly good clothes that were out of season.

One time, someone called and said he had 152,000 pounds of candy — four big truckloads — to give away. Could Ranya Kelly find people who wanted it? Of course she could. She gets calls every day. And now she distributes more than $1,000,000 worth of merchandise and food every year, all because one day she decided to look for a big box to send a package to a friend.

What Can I Do?

THE OVERSTOCK MITZVAH

"Do you donate overstock?" It's an easy question to ask. Many storekeepers don't think about doing it, and are never asked. If you ask at a bakery, or shoe store, or toy store, make sure the owner understands you are not asking for current stock. You only want things they are going to throw out. . .two-day old donuts, out-of-style shoes, games that have been opened, books with bent pages, or perfectly good things they are throwing out because they need storage space for new stock.

You will be astounded at how much food and merchandise can be distributed from even a single store, usually as a result of one person's efforts. You can be that one person.

For many merchants, the problem is pick-up and distribution. Teen-agers who can drive, younger kids who have bikes, and neighbors who have vans can join you in this mitzvah.

THE BABY CORNER

Sometimes when you walk into a synagogue, you see a big food barrel. People bring in cans, boxes, and bags of food which are taken to soup kitchens, shelters, and food banks so that hungry people will no longer be hungry. Having a barrel in the synagogue makes it easier for people to do the mitzvah of sharing food. If they have a meeting, or they are coming to religious school, they can bring some tuna or cereal or canned soup and drop it gently into the barrel.

And sometimes next to the food barrel is a crib with a big sign on it saying, "Mitzvah Crib" or "Baby Corner."

One day, a few years back in Seattle, Washington, a woman named Jeannie Jaybush was surprised to read how many poor children and babies there were in her city. Some of them didn't even have a home. Maybe one or both of their parents couldn't find a job, had lost their job, or worked hard but couldn't make enough money to live decently.

Instead of just being sad, Jeannie decided to do something about what she had learned. She asked if she could set up a crib in her church building to collect things for needy infants. Her church agreed that it was a good idea, and as soon as the Baby Corner was set up, people began to bring in all kinds of things: baby food and formula, diapers and baby powder, blankets and clothing and playpens and strollers and car seats. They also brought toys and stuffed animals, because they know babies and children need to play, too. It was easy for many of the people. Their children were grown and these things were just sitting in their basement, garage, or attic.

Others made a special trip to the store to buy new blankets or toys or clothes. Even little children gave away some of their toys and dolls.

Every time the crib filled up, Jeannie and her friends took the baby things to shelters and soup kitchens for people who needed them.

One day a big truck pulled up in front of the church. It was a very big truck, one of those you see on the highways with 18 wheels and room for lots of things. The driver unloaded cartons and cartons of diapers, about 11,000 diapers in all. Somebody had heard about the Mitzvah Crib and decided to give the diapers, but whoever it was didn't want anyone to know. Some people like to do mitzvahs secretly.

One of Jeannie's friends spoke about the crib to some Jewish teachers who were in Seattle for a convention. They decided to put cribs in their synagogues back home.

Some day we hope there won't be any food barrels or mitzvah cribs in synagogues or churches. Some day we hope all babies and children will have everything they need to be healthy and happy.

What Can I Do?

A MITZVAH CRIB

You and your friends can help set up a mitzvah crib in your synagogue or school. Start by getting someone to lend a crib. Then make lists of the things you want to collect, little things such as: diapers, formula, baby food, clothes, blankets, toys, stuffed animals, pacifiers, baby soap, and shampoo. And big items such as high chairs, play pens, and car seats.

Post the list on the crib and on the synagogue bulletin board, and send copies home with nursery and religious school students. Ask the Sisterhood and Brotherhood to publish the list in monthly bulletins, and remind people of the project at their meetings. Find a shelter or agency that works with needy families, and as the crib fills up, arrange to deliver the contents.

BUTTERCUP AND SWEET PEA

I met my first clown a few years ago. His name was Buttons, and I guess he was in disguise that day because he looked perfectly normal to me. But he showed me a picture of himself with a round red nose, a puffy clown suit, and very big shoes.

Next I met Panda, and then I just started bumping into clowns all over the place. About six months ago I met Buttercup and Sweet Pea.

They were also in disguise, wearing their regular clothes and acting just like you and me.

Buttons and Panda and Buttercup and Sweet Pea all like to make people happy. They probably have millions of smiles and laughs and warm hugs packed away in their memories from the hours they have spent being clowns.

My clown friends have learned how to juggle, to tie balloons into animal shapes, and to do magic tricks, not just because it's fun, but because they can go to hospitals or old age homes or shelters and entertain people. Sometimes they will even teach people how to juggle or make balloon animals, or do a magic trick, so that after they leave, these people can practice and then go off on their own and make others smile.

One day Buttercup and Sweet Pea came up with a wonderful idea: They taught a class in clowning in their synagogue's religious school. They must have said to themselves, "Why should someone wait until he or she is 25 or 40 or 53 to become a clown? Let's start them off early, so they can make more people happy." And when they had finished taking the class, the students all went to a hospital to entertain the patients, so many more people wound up with smiles on their faces that day.

What Can I Do?

USE YOUR TALENTS TO MAKE PEOPLE HAPPY

Everyone knows that you have to learn Hebrew in religious school, as well as Jewish history, and all about Shabbat and the holidays and about Israel. And, of course, you have to prepare to become a Bar or Bat Mitzvah. But wouldn't it be wonderful if everyone also learned how to be a clown! Think of all the lonely people who wouldn't be lonely anymore, and all the sad people who wouldn't be sad anymore if we had hundreds or thousands of Hebrew school students out there clowning.

So invite a local clown to teach your class or youth group how to tumble, or juggle, or make balloon animals. And take your act on the road.

Clowning isn't the only way to make people smile. Do you play the guitar, can you sing, do you like to tell jokes? Think of how you and your friends can make people happy.

It's like using one candle to light another one, and then another, until there are hundreds of them burning. All that light takes away a lot of darkness.

I think Buttercup and Sweet Pea are on to something.

THE POTATO PEOPLE

Not long ago, Ray Buchanan and Ken Horne found out that some farmers in Virginia had a lot of potatoes they couldn't use. They were too hard to harvest, too small to sell to the markets, or they looked a little funny, although they were perfectly good to eat. Ray and Ken knew that many hungry people in America would enjoy eating these potatoes. All they had to do was get them from the farmer's fields to the hungry people's dinner tables.

So they started The Potato Project, and found it was not so difficult to work out ways to get giant trucks to load up the potatoes and take them to food banks.

This sounds like a great new idea, but it's really very old. It's the mitzvah of *leket*, which means gleaning. For at least 3,000 years, Jewish farmers have left some of the crops in their fields unpicked, so hungry people could come and take what they need. There are two other mitzvahs that go along with *leket*. *Peah* requires farmers to leave the corners of their fields unpicked, and *shichecha* means that if, for some reason, a farmer forgets to take in some of the harvested crops, they also must be left for poor people.

Everyone doing *leket* in Virginia is happy these days. The farmer is happy because the potatoes aren't left in the fields to go to waste, and the hungry people are happy because they have healthy things to eat.

And Ray Buchanan and Ken Horne are happy because last year alone they managed to get about 22 million pounds of potatoes and other vegetables to people.

Since they began, the total is 142,000,000 pounds of food. WOW!

TEMPLE BETH AM

What Can I Do?

BE A GLEANER

You — and friends in your school or synagogue — can do the mitzvah of *leket*. Ask a nearby farmer to tell you when he or she has finished harvesting the main portion of his crops. Then organize a group to go out to the farm to pick the leftovers. Deliver your harvest to a local food bank or soup kitchen.

If you have fruit trees or a vegetable garden of your own, pick some of the oranges, apples, tomatoes, or peppers to give away to kitchens that feed the hungry.

Encourage your synagogue to plant a garden right on its own land. Then help to harvest all the vegetables for poor people.

ZALMAN'S AUNT MINNIE
AND THE MATTRESS MAN

I never met Zalman's Aunt Minnie. She died long ago, but I feel like I knew her because of the wonderful story my friend Zalman told me about her.

Zalman's Aunt Minnie loved old people very much. She liked to talk to them and visit with them and do things with them. If they couldn't get out and do their own shopping, she would pick up things at the grocery store. If they felt lonely, she would buy little things to make them happier, such as flowers or a pretty card or a calendar with pictures of Israel. She liked doing these things because she really loved old people.

One day, a big mitzvah came her way. When she went to one of the old age homes, she saw that the mattresses the people slept on were very old. So she went to a man who sold mattresses and asked him to give her 50 of them for the people at the home. The man, who liked Aunt Minnie and also liked doing mitzvahs, said he would be happy to.

Then Zalman's Aunt Minnie asked, "Can you show me the mattresses?" He said, "Of course," and took her into a big storeroom.

You would think Aunt Minnie would have been happy to see all those mattresses, but she wasn't. They were the kind of mattresses they have at camp — the thin ones with stripes and buttons. So Zalman's Aunt Minnie asked the mattress man, "What kind of mattress do *you* sleep on?". He took her to a different part of the storeroom and showed her mattresses that were thicker, and nicer, and more comfortable.

Zalman's Aunt Minnie said, "You know old people have old bones. They need thicker mattresses. I will need 50 of these more comfortable mattresses."

The mattress man must have been very surprised at Zalman's Aunt Minnie, but he understood that she was right. He wanted to do a mitzvah, but he hadn't thought hard enough about how to do it the best way possible. Once he realized what the old people needed, he agreed to give her 50 of the better mattresses.

And for years, many old people slept very well because of Zalman's Aunt Minnie.

When I lie down on my big, soft mattress at night, I hope that everyone sleeps comfortably, so we can all wake up rested, and ready to do more mitzvahs.

What Can I Do?

HIDDUR MITZVAH

When we have some place important to go, we make sure to look our best.

And when we do mitzvahs, we should do them with a special touch. That's called *hiddur mitzvah*, making mitzvahs beautiful.

Zalman's Aunt Minnie knew about hiddur mitzvah. She wanted the mattress man to donate not just any old mattresses, but ones that were comfortable for the old people.

When you do your mitzvahs, think about how you can do them in the best way possible.

If you set up a mitzvah crib or food barrel in your school, decorate it and put up colorful signs telling what to put in. That way people will want to contribute.

If you are collecting toys or used clothing for a shelter, make sure that all the toys work, that the puzzles have all their pieces, and that the clothes are clean.

If you are taking food and clothing to a shelter, remember to add some candy, books, or flowers. People who are having a hard time financially enjoy a treat just like everyone else.

THE EAGLE REPAIR SHOP

Did you know that eagles can catch pneumonia?

I didn't. . .until I met Sigrid Ueblacker. I met her, as I so often meet Mitzvah People, by reading an article about her. That's when I learned you could do mitzvahs not only with people, but with animals, too.

Sigrid knows a lot about many kinds of birds — barn owls and screech owls, Mississippi kites and prairie falcons, red-tailed hawks and golden eagles. She knows about them because she takes care of them when they are sick.

Yes, birds get sick, too.

Sometimes they are injured when they are caught in a storm, or they fly into cars or trucks or fences by mistake. Other times they eat things that aren't good for them. And sometimes they are injured by people.

After I read about Sigrid, I decided to visit her the

next time I was in Denver. A friend drove me a long
way out of town where I saw huge bird cages, maybe
400 feet long and 50 feet high. They were the biggest
bird cages I had ever seen. This is where Sigrid does
her mitzvah work. She calls her place The Birds of
Prey Rehabilitation Foundation. I call it The Eagle
Repair Shop.

Sigrid's work is really very simple. She finds injured wild birds and with the help of friends and veterinarians, she does what she can to make them better. Sometimes other people find injured birds and bring them to her. A couple of years ago, she was able to let four magnificent bald eagles go home to the sky and mountains. They were named Hope and Thunder and Spirit and Hamlet. Everyone was so happy when they were let free. It was a little like when the Children of Israel left Egypt thousands of years ago. Sigrid taught me that freedom is as important to birds as it is to us.

But sometimes even though the birds get better, they are not strong enough to live safely in the outside world, so Sigrid has to keep them in the giant cages at The Eagle Repair Shop. One is a red-tailed hawk she calls Chanute. Sometimes she takes Chanute to schools and libraries to teach people how to love and respect the great wild birds of this earth.

The next time you look up in the sky and see beautiful birds soaring on the wind, or swooping down to the branch of a big tree, think about Thunder or Spirit or Hope or another bird Sigrid has saved, and remember how important it is to be free.

What Can I Do?

MITZVAH BIRD PROJECT

When I was young, I had all kinds of pets. . .cats, dogs and hamsters, parakeets and a parrot, and once I had three ducks I called Huey, Dewey, and Louie. Animals and birds keep people company and make them smile.

Birds make especially good mitzvah pets, because they don't need to be walked or played with. And people in hospitals and old age homes, or elderly people who live alone might love to have a bird to watch and listen to. . .and even chat with.

Ask around for unused cages that may be gathering dust in someone's attic. Then see if a pet store owner will donate a couple of finches, or a parakeet or two. Check with a nursing home or hospital to see if they will let residents keep pets in their rooms, or in the dining hall or sitting room. If the residents or patients can't take care of the birds, make sure that someone on staff is willing to feed them and clean their cages, and try to come yourself now and again to visit.

If you have a dog or cat, find out if a nursing home or hospital in your area has a visiting pet program. Arrange to visit once a week with your pet. Bring along his or her favorite toys, so the people can play with your pet and watch it do tricks.

THE PENNY HARVEST

When I first heard about Teddy Gross, he was known as the 7 million penny man.

The 7 million pennies weren't really his, though some were. Most he got from his neighbors. And he didn't keep the pennies. They were for tzedakah.

Teddy lives in one of those tall apartment buildings in Manhattan, so you can imagine how many neighbors he has. . .hundreds, maybe even thousands! And one day in January of 1991, Teddy just started asking them for their pennies. When he was through, he counted them, rolled them up, put them in the bank, and then used the money for homeless and poor people in the city.

He never imagined getting more than a few thousand pennies. But 7 million is how many he got on the first round of what he calls the "Penny Harvest," and it didn't take him long to do it. That was $70,000 for mitzvahs.

In November 1992, Teddy got 327 New York City schools to harvest pennies. They collected 20 tons of coins worth $89,706.01, which was distributed to 11 different mitzvah projects, worldwide. By April 1993, Teddy and over 1,000 volunteers had gathered 33,000,000 pennies. And now the project has a name — Common Cents.

People don't think pennies can buy a lot nowadays. Your grandparents may tell you they used to buy a newspaper for a penny and a candy bar or a soda cost only a few pennies.

But Teddy Gross knows better than anyone how a few pennies here and a few pennies there can add up to big mitzvahs. . .even today!

What Can I Do?

YOU CAN BE A
MILLION PENNY PERSON

I have 22 pushkas. People know I collect them, so they give them to me as presents. Some just say "tzedakah", one says "Tzedakah Makes a Difference," and the one with Snoopy on top of his doghouse, says, "Tzedakah Isn't Peanuts!" They are metal, plastic, cardboard, and clay. One looks like a giant Hershey Kiss, another has little bears on the side. I try to put some money in one of them every day, and often when my friends come over, they do, too.

Start with your tzedakah box at home. Drop in a coin each morning before you go to school. Keep your eyes open for coins people drop on the street.

Put an extra tzedakah box near the washing machine. Whoever does laundry can collect the coins left in clothes pockets and drop them in the box.

And don't be afraid to check under the couch pillows once in awhile. And don't be afraid to ask your friends or family, visitors or neighbors for their extra pennies.

Remind them that pennies become food and blankets and baseball gloves and wheelchairs for people who need them.

MITZVAH DOGS

Everyday people think of new ways to do mitzvahs. Sometimes they are taking a walk, and they get a mitzvah idea, or they are sitting in a chair on their front porch, and a mitzvah idea comes into their head.

Think about seeing-eye dogs. You may have noticed one walking beside a blind person, showing the person when to cross the street, or when to stop for traffic. Or maybe you saw one sitting in a park relaxing with its owner.

About 100 years ago, someone got the idea that dogs could help blind people. And about 20 years ago, a woman named Bonnie Bergin thought of a newer way that dogs can help people. She calls her dogs SERVICE dogs. They are mitzvah dogs who work with people in wheelchairs.

SERVICE dogs are great picker-uppers if the person drops something. They turn light switches off when it is time for the person to go to bed. They press elevator buttons. They help with the shopping. And, they can even pull wheelchairs. In fact, the dogs know how to do 89 different things.

And they have wonderful names like Kosmic and Barnum and Da Vinci and Daffodil. I met one named "Garfield," which I thought was supposed to be the name of a cat. But it didn't seem to bother the dog. He just went on doing his work, picking up things, pressing elevator buttons, and pulling his owner's wheelchair.

Mitzvah dogs are easy to pick out in a crowd: they all wear backpacks. If you happen to get close enough, you'll hear their owners say, "Good Boy!" or "Good Girl!" after they have done one of their jobs well.

One of the best things about the Mitzvah dogs is that people like to come up and pet the dogs and talk to the owners about themselves. Some people are afraid to talk to people who use wheelchairs, but the Mitzvah dogs make it easier.

But remember to ask permission to pet the dog. You don't want to bother the dog when it's working.

There are now 40 programs around the country training SERVICE dogs for people with disabilities.

If you spend a little time every day thinking, maybe you'll invent a new mitzvah that will make life better for people, just like Bonnie Bergin did when she came up with the idea for SERVICE dogs.

What Can I Do?

A LARGE-PRINT BOOK

One way to work with individuals with disabilities is to make sure that your synagogue provides all kinds of access.

For example, you and your family may want to use some tzedakah money to purchase large print or braille prayer books for visually-impaired people. There are also communications devices so hearing-impaired people can participate in services. Some synagogues hire sign language interpreters one Shabbat a month or at High Holiday time. A simple, removeable ramp at the door may make it possible for people who use wheelchairs or walkers to get in more easily.

THE MAN WHO WARMS
MANY HEARTS AND BONES

Warren M. Toltz of Denver is someone I'd like to meet. What he does is nothing fancy. He doesn't sell big boats, and he doesn't design computers. Yet he takes his job seriously and does it well, with lots of mitzvahs in mind.

Mr. Toltz owns one of Colorado's largest and oldest dry cleaning chains. His 24 stores are filled with noisy machines, hot irons, racks of shirts, pants, dresses, and draperies. . .and customers.

Denver, like most of America's cities, has many poor people and more than its share of homeless individuals. Winters can be very cold in Colorado, and many residents don't have money to buy coats. This is where Mr. Toltz's mitzvah comes in.

In 1980, one of his customers, Elizabeth Yanish, began collecting coats for people who couldn't afford them. Early on, she realized that if she had several drop-off points, she could collect many more coats, and many more people would benefit.

A year later, Mr. Toltz got involved. Dependable Cleaners became the sponsor of what is now Colorado's largest coat drive. In that first year, using the dry-cleaning stores as drop-off points, Coats 4 Colorado collected and distributed 850 coats. The project was small enough so that Mr. Toltz could clean the coats, and even replace a button or two. Since then, the coat project has grown and is now collecting up to 50,000 coats a year. That's a total of more than 250,000 overcoats and raincoats, trench coats and parkas, down coats and wool coats, grey coats and red coats. . .and bright green ones, too.

After the coats are collected, Coats 4 Colorado has a giant, two-day coat giveaway project, when the coats are distributed to shelters, organizations that work with poor and homeless people, and just plain people who need a coat.

Now, because of Mr. Toltz and his Coats 4 Colorado volunteers, thousands of people in Denver are no longer afraid of winter. They can go to work or school, or to the store, without shivering or catching cold. They can be nice and warm until the glorious Colorado spring arrives, and they can go outside without a coat.

What Can I Do?

MITZVAH TOOLS

For Mr. Toltz, his dry-cleaning machine was a mitzvah tool. He dry-cleaned thousands of coats distributed through the Coats 4 Colorado project. Think of all the other tools and instruments that can be used for mitzvahs.

You can play piano just for fun, but you can also play to cheer up people who may be lonely. A guitar is good for that, too, or a violin or clarinet, though a tuba may be too loud. We use hammers for fixing bikes or toys, but we can also use them to help repair someone's house that was damaged in a flood or fire, or to build a sukkah for someone unable to build one.

Cars can be mitzvah tools, when we use them to deliver food packages or take elderly people who no longer drive on errands or to synagogue. The same goes for trucks and airplanes. . .or bikes. All of them can be tools for mitzvahs.

One of my favorite mitzvah tools is the computer. Does your computer have a name? Some people with Macintosh computers call them "Mac;" those who have IBM's call them "I" names like Izzy or Iris or Indiana Jones.

Think how many ways you can use Mac or Indiana Jones to do mitzvahs:

Keep a list of your friends who like to do mitzvahs and what mitzvahs they like to do. When it's time to do one of those mitzvahs, you'll know whom to call.

Design a flyer to remind people to bring food to the synagogue food barrel, or clothes and toys to the Mitzvah Crib.

Keep track of how much tzedakah money you have collected and where you gave it.

Teach someone else how to use the computer. Many older people, especially, feel left behind because they never learned how. Teach them to write letters, design birthday cards for their grandchildren, write stories about their lives, or even play games. Computers are getting small enough to carry. Maybe the students in your math class or computer club can take their computers to a retirement or nursing home and teach the people how to use them.

THE WOMAN WHO COLLECTS
WEDDING DRESSES

Some people collect coins.

Other people collect stamps, baseball cards, dolls, flags, or teacups. If they are rich, they may even collect old cars like 1938 Rolls Royces or 1949 Jaguars.

In Jerusalem, there's a woman who collects wedding dresses. She is the Rabbanit Bracha Kapach, and most people call her "The Rabbanit," though her friends call her "Bracha" which means "a blessing". So many people know her in Jerusalem, that sometimes you can get in a taxicab and say, "I want to go to the Rabbanit's house," and the driver will know just where it is.

The Rabbanit does so many mitzvahs every week, it is hard to count them. She gets Shabbat food for people who don't have enough money for challah or wine. She runs a summer camp for the kids in her neighborhood. Sometimes she finds jobs for people who don't have work. She even stores clothes in a big room underneath her apartment so people who need clothes can come and get some.

One of her favorite mitzvahs is weddings. She loves weddings. I think by now she must have been to hundreds of them. Wedding dresses cost a lot to buy or rent, and some brides don't have enough money. Since the Rabbanit decided to collect wedding dresses, brides who thought they would have to get married in a regular dress can choose a gown from the Rabbanit's huge closet.

There are long dresses and short dresses, ones with flowers and ones without, some with veils and some with no veils. The Rabbanit has a wonderful collection because all kinds of people give them to her knowing she will use them to make brides very happy on their wedding day.

It doesn't cost the bride anything, and a day or two after the wedding she brings the gown back to the Rabbanit, so another bride can wear it.

If the bride and groom don't have much money, the Rabbanit also will arrange for food — especially a nice wedding cake — a photographer, and musicians. And sometimes when the bride and groom don't have many friends or relatives, the Rabbanit invites lots of her own friends so there will be a nice crowd to sing and dance and celebrate.

The Rabbanit's wedding mitzvahs don't even end there. She sometimes collects dishes and silverware and glasses and sheets and pillow cases and other things a couple needs to set up their new home. And the nice thing is, as time goes on, if the bride and groom start to make money, they come back to join the Rabbanit in her mitzvah work.

When you sit in her living room, the Rabbanit will show you photo albums of the weddings and tell you how all the brides and grooms are doing. But don't be surprised if right in the middle of a sentence, the phone rings or someone knocks on the door to see her. It's always something about mitzvahs.

So the next time you look at your baseball cards or you see a collection of tea cups, think of the Rabbanit Kapach and her collection of wedding dresses.

What a nice mitzvah it is to make brides happy on their wedding day!

What Can I Do?

SAY IT WITH ROSES

Weddings bring to mind some simple mitzvahs you can do. Check with your rabbi to see who has scheduled a wedding at the synagogue. Call the people and ask if you can have some of the flowers when it's over. Then you can take a rose or two to someone who is sick or lives alone, or several bunches of flowers to the residents of a nursing home or hospital. Think how much brighter their day will be!

And when you deliver the flowers, maybe the person will invite you to sit and chat a little. You may find a new friend, because of a few roses.

You can do this with Bar and Bat Mitzvah flowers, Shabbat pulpit flowers, and even those used to celebrate a birthday or anniversary.

THE BAT MITZVAH MITZVAH

Elana Erdstein's Bat Mitzvah project started with a wicker basket of little soaps and lotions that her grandmother kept in the bathroom—leftovers from vacations and trips. When Elana saw them, she made a mitzvah connection. "What if I start to collect them," she thought, "and deliver them to shelters and food banks."

She began by asking friends and neighbors, writing letters, making phone calls, and circulating a flyer that asked:

- When you travel, do you ever stay at hotels that give you sample-size shampoo, lotion, sewing kits, etc?
- Do you take them home with you, whether or not you need them?

Elana set up collection boxes in her synagogue, other synagogues and churches, even the library. She was invited to present her project to a dental convention and was loaded down with toothbrushes and floss. Hotels and cosmetic companies sent her deodorants, aspirin, facial tissue, and hair coloring. By the time she had celebrated her Bat Mitzvah, she had collected 25,000 items, worth over $15,000. Once or twice a week, Elana and her mother picked up the toiletries and delivered them — to a battered women's shelter, a drug rehab center for teens, and an emergency food bank.

Elana intends to continue her efforts, and is preparing a start-up kit to encourage others to start their own programs. It takes planning, she points out, but it doesn't cost anything except postage and gas.

Most important, Elana learned that mitzvah power is a wonderful thing, and that you don't have to wait until you're 27 or 57 to make a big difference in the lives of many people.

"Knowing that I can help other people is the best feeling. If you help other kids to get that feeling, I think the results will last all our lives," she wrote.

If thousands of young people would make a mitzvah connection like Elana did, the world would get better that much quicker.

What Can I Do?

THE SHAMPOO MITZVAH

Did you know that you cannot use food stamps to purchase toiletries? That's why providing homeless people, food banks, and shelters with shampoo, soap, toothpaste, and shower caps is an important mitzvah.

Begin by asking your friends and family to clean out their medicine chests. Even if you get only 10 or 20 items to bring to a food bank, you have made a difference.

If you want to do more, call some shelters and food banks and find out what specific non-food items they need. Then ask if you can set up a collection box in your synagogue, and make an announcement at services or synagogue meetings. You can even write to neighborhood stores and banks to let them know about your mitzvah project and ask them to become collection points.

If you want to do even more than that, ask dentists, doctors, hairdressers, and pharmacists for samples. And you can contact hotels or cosmetic companies to contribute as well.

If they say, "no," well, you tried. If they say, "yes," you will have even more lotion and sewing kits to donate.

When it comes to mitzvahs, it never hurts to ask.

THE MITZVAH JUST WAITING
TO HAPPEN

This is the story of six fifth-graders at the Krieger Solomon Schechter School in Baltimore who have started something which could become an Unbelievably Giant Mitzvah.

One of them, Ashlie Levy, noticed each day at the end of lunch that her classmates threw away perfectly good food — leftover apples and oranges, boxes of raisins, and unopened cans of juice.

Then her teacher, Fern Weiner, told the class about another Mitzvah Hero, Steve Chaikin, a local law student. Steve got permission from the Baltimore Orioles to collect leftover food at the stadium after each game, and deliver it to shelters and soup kitchens. From this initial effort, Steve expanded his activities when he and his friend Mark Iorio founded Project Hunger.

This gave Ashlie an idea. She enlisted three friends, Maia Aronson, Ashley Katz, and Tova Reichel, and the three set up colorful boxes at the lunchroom doors.

Later, they were joined by two other classmates, Elizabeth Levin and Lauren Kaye. Each day they make an announcement encouraging students to place uneaten food in the boxes. The food is sorted, perishables are refrigerated, and each Friday one or two students and parents take it to a food bank for distribution.

Think of all the good food that has been saved. And think of how much more could be saved if other schools — public and private, elementary and high schools — would begin to collect leftover lunch food each day.

It was a mitzvah waiting to happen. All it took was for someone to say, "Why don't we do it!" Suddenly all kinds of good things began to happen. And they could happen so many other places, too.

What Can I Do?

THE LEFTOVER MITZVAH

Collecting leftover food — from school lunchrooms, youth group meetings, Bar and Bat Mitzvah parties, weddings, and sports events — is a mitzvah waiting to happen anytime, anywhere. But you have to remember that food is perishable. Some food packages have expiration dates on them, and meat, dairy, and fruits and vegetables can last only a certain amount of time before they are no longer safe to eat. State laws and Health Department rules in each community give guidelines on safe recycling of food. Ask at your local shelter or soup kitchen for a copy of your city's laws concerning food donations. Your parents, teachers, or youth group leaders should carefully review them with you before you begin your "Leftover Project."

Don't be discouraged if you save only six boxes of raisins or three bags of pretzels a day. It is food that will feed hungry people.

MITZVAH HEROES

Did you read about the basketball player who gives tzedakah to buy uniforms and basketballs for poor kids? Or the rock star who visits sick kids in the hospital?

They're famous because they're stars; they're heroes because they do mitzvahs. And when famous people do mitzvahs their fans will want to do them, too. I like that.

But you don't have to be famous to be a mitzvah hero.

Mitzvah heroes are short and tall, young and old. I read about a 12-year old who collected beat-up, old bicycles, fixed and painted them, and gave them away to kids who didn't have enough money for a bike. I know an eye doctor who goes to Mexico twice a year and operates on blind people so they get their sight back. He does this as a volunteer. And I know a lawyer who loves to cook, who prepares meals for people who live alone. They do their work quietly. They don't brag, and they don't seek publicity.

And they are easy to find.

Look around and ask, "Who is doing mitzvahs?" Your parents, teachers, neighbors will know one or two or maybe even more. Then find a way to meet them and find out how you can join in their work.

TIKKUN OLAM

Our world is broken in big and small ways, and when we do mitzvahs, we are fixing it up! That's called *Tikkun Olam*, "repairing the world." When we are young we can do small mitzvahs to fix small things that are broken. When we get older, we can do bigger things. And if we ever become a sports star or a corporate executive we can do big time fixing up.

Even if you're very young, you can begin to do wonderful things for people. You don't have to wait until you are older, until you can drive, or vote, or have a high school diploma. You can start right now.

This week, select a few cans of food from the pantry to drop in the Food Barrel at your synagogue.

In a few years, when you can drive, you can be the one to organize a group of friends to collect the barrels and take them down to a shelter.

And if you ever become a rock star, you can ask the thousands of people who come to your concert to bring cans of food for the hungry. That would be a pretty awesome mitzvah.

But you need to start practicing now, because small and medium-sized mitzvahs make a big difference.

And remember to say, "not yet," when you see people doing big-time mitzvahs. "Not yet, but someday soon." Someday you'll be doing them, too. You'll be a big time fixer-upper for the world!

ABOUT THE AUTHOR

Danny Siegel, a 1993 recipient of the prestigious Covenant Award for Exceptional Jewish Educators, has been described as "American Jewry's leading expert in microphilanthropy." As chairman of Ziv Tzedakah Fund, which he founded 17 years ago, he has collected nearly $2 million for grass-roots community projects worldwide. He lectures to synagogues, federations, religious schools, and university student groups about the dozens of mitzvah people he has met, and encourages his audiences to get involved. When not on the road, Danny lives, works, and writes in Rockville, MD. He is the author of 18 books of prose and poetry. This is his first book for children.

ABOUT THE ILLUSTRATOR

Judith Friedman lives in Illinois with her husband David and their three cats, Amanda, Adele, and Celia. She studied art in her native France, and when she arrived in this country at the age of 17, continued to study at the Art Institute of Chicago, where she later taught. Judith has illustrated several children's books, including *Jeremy's Dreidel* for Kar-Ben. She also accepts commissions to paint children's portraits.

For more information about these and other mitzvah heroes, contact Ziv Tzedakah Fund, Inc., 263 Congressional Lane, #708, Rockville, MD 20852.